Glimpses of the Indian Economy

Ratan Lal Basu

Glimpses of the Indian Economy

Ratan Lal Basu

Published by Kautilya, 2023.

GLIMPSES OF THE INDIAN ECONOMY

First edition. January 30, 2023.

ISBN: 979-8215874653

Written by Ratan Lal Basu.

Contents

Chapter-1: Diversification of Agriculture in India and the Poor

Introduction

The question of diversification of agriculture in India, especially in Eastern India, has become an important topic for discussion and debate in recent years. In fact, it is held by many economists and politicians that poverty and unemployment (both open and disguised) in the rural sector in Eastern India are the consequences of low production and productivity in agriculture. One common phrase, very often used by politico-economic announcements is: "Diversification in agriculture is the panacea for low productivity, poverty and unemployment in the agricultural and rural sector." In most of the cases, however, the spokesmen for diversification hardly provide any definition of the term 'diversification'.

In general sense, diversification of agriculture may mean:

i) Diversification between agriculture and allied activities like animal husbandry, fishing etc. and/or

ii) Diversification in cropping pattern

The second category may be subdivided into:

a) Diversification between food crops and non-food crops

b) Diversification between cereals and non-cereal food crops

c) Diversification between traditional crops and horticulture, and

d) Diversification between low productivity to high productivity crops

In this article we confine our study to the second category, viz. diversification in cropping pattern in the four senses mentioned above.

All the eleven States of the eastern zone are characterized by diversity of climatic, soil and topographical conditions allowing for cultivation of all varieties of crops. All these States are characterized by adequate water resources and fertile soil. There are no dearth of rainfall and bright sunshine in most of the States and all varieties of soil (alluvial, laterite, rocky etc.) are to be found in most of these States. In brief, nature has provided this region with ample opportunities for production of all conceivable varieties of agricultural crops.

Agricultural production in this region on the whole is characterized by the predominance of traditional pre-capitalistic farming in tiny holdings. As a consequence, productivity is low and in most of the cases meant for subsistence of the poor farmers. Naturally, for most of the States, the dominant crops are cereals, especially rice (paddy), which is the major cereal food crop for this zone taken as a whole.

Under the present circumstances, there is wide scope for diversification of agricultural production of this region in all the four senses mentioned above. But we are to remember that, in a market-oriented economy as conceived under the New Economic Policy of 1991, direction of crop diversification ought to be guided by market forces, especially, demand conditions, mainly export demand. So, without expanding and sustainable export opportunities, substantial crop diversification is not possible simply depending on home demand. Secondly, from the supply side, crop diversification calls for adequate supply of inputs (seeds, fertilizers, pesticides, irrigation facilities etc.) and credit facilities.

Taking for granted that all the favorable demand and supply criteria have been met, the question arises who are going to be the real beneficiaries of diversification, or more specifically, whether diversification is going to reduce poverty and unemployment in the rural sector of the eleven States of the eastern zone.

This article is going to take up this all important issue. But to start with, we are to take a brief glimpse of the ancient practice of crop-diversification as prescribed in the Arthaśāstra of Kautilya. This has a special significance for a seminar held at Patna. In fact, the first politically unified India (the Magadha Empire (beginning from the reign of Ajātaśatru and culminating in the Mauryan Empire) had its capital in this city (then called Pātaliputra) and the guiding principle of that Empire was the Arthaśāstra of Kautilya. Besides the excellent prescriptions in this text for crop-diversification to facilitate eco-friendly and sustainable agricultural development, we should also look into its opposite, the forced commercialization and diversification during British rule and its horrible consequences for the poor. This may serve as a caution to the blind adherents of the policy of agricultural diversification today.

Crop Diversification in the Arthaśāstra

The Arthaśāstra of Kautilya prescribes crop-diversification on the basis of diversity of climatic, topographical and soil conditions, keeping in view the requirements of food, fodder and industrial raw materials, and the preservation of environment and ecology, especially, fertility of soil. Kautilya's prescriptions are discussed in brief in the following.

How various crops are to be cultivated are described in detail in II/24 of the Arthaśāstra of Kautilya. Here Kautilya describes how different crops are to be planted according to the specificity of soil and weather conditions. Varieties of the same crops (depending on specific conditions) are also mentioned. On the whole agriculture, according to Kautilya, is to be eco-friendly and sustainable; and there should be a proper balance among different kinds of uses of scarce land.

All varieties of seeds are to be collected in proper time and preserved properly.

To quote:

2/24/1: The Director of Agriculture, himself conversant with the practice of agriculture, water-divining and the science of rearing plants, or assisted by experts in these, should collect, in the proper seasons, seeds of all kinds of grains, flowers, fruits, vegetables, bulbous roots, roots, creeper fruits, flax, and cotton.

Crops are to be sown according to appropriateness of soils, climatic conditions etc.

To quote:

2/24/2: He should cause them to be sown in land, suitable for each, which has been ploughed many times, through serfs, labourers and persons paying off their fines by personal labour.

2/24/11: In conformity with that, he should cause crops to be sown, requiring plenty of water or little water.

2/24/15: Or, the sowing of seeds (should be) in conformity with the season.

2/24/19: According to the amount of water (available) for the work, he should decide on wet crops, winter crops or summer crops.

2/24/22: (A region) where the foam strikes (the banks) is (suited) for creeper fruits, (regions on) the outskirts of overflows, for long pepper, grapes and sugarcanes, (those on) the borders of wells, for vegetables and roots, (those on) the borders of moist beds of lakes, for green grasses, ridges for plants reaped by cutting, (such as) perfume-plants, medicinal herbs, uśīra-grass, hrībera, pindāluka and others.

2/24/23: And on lands suitable for each, he should raise plants that grow on dry lands and that grow in wet-lands.

The proper condition for growth of crops is described in the following ślokas.

2/24/10: Where it rains distributing wind and sunshine properly and creating three (periods for the drying of) cowdung cakes, there the growth of crops is certain.

Kautilya describes the order of crops to be grown so as to maintain a balance in fertility of soil and ecology. To quote:

2/24/12: śāli-rice, vrīhi-rice, kodrava, sesamum, priyańgu, udāraka and varaka are the first sowings.

2/24/13: mudga, māsa and śaimbya are the middle sowings.

2/24/14: Safflower, lentils, kulattha, barley, wheat, kalāya, linseed and mustard are the last sowings.

Kautilya also describes how seeds are to be prepared before sowing, and how crop saplings are to be properly maintained. To quote:

2/24/24: Soaking in the dew (by night) and drying in the heat (by day) for seven days and nights (is the treatment) in the case of seeds of grains, for three days and nights or five in the case of seeds of pulses, smearing at the cut with honey, ghee and pig's fat, mixed with cowdung in the case of stalks that serve as seeds, (smearing) with honey and ghee in the case of bulbous roots, smearing with cowdung in the case of stone-like seeds, (and) in the case of trees, burning in the pit and fulfillment of the longing with cow-bones and cowdung at the proper time.

2/24/25: And when hey have sprouted, he should feed them with fresh acrid fish along with the milk of the snuhi-plant (Kangle 1986).

Crop Diversification during British Regime

Before the advent of the British in India, the country was divided into a large number of independent political units. The British invaded, subjugated and unified them to form the vast British Indian Empire. With the emergence of modern industries in Britain in course of the industrial revolution, India became the major source of raw materials for British industries. To fulfill this requirement, the British government undertook commercialization of agriculture in India so as to guide Indian agricultural production according to the requirements of British industries.

The process took various forms: tea and coffee plantations, indigo cultivation, cultivation of cotton and jute. Opening up of the Suez Canal and expansion of railways in India facilitated this process. As a matter of fact, the entire process of this commercialization was forced on the poor farmers, either by direct coercion as in case of indigo cultivation, or indirectly through British revenue administration. Although a class of native traders and money lenders (who co-operate with the British to accentuate the process of commercialization) was considerably benefited, the consequences for the poor were devastating. One of the most important causes of recurrent famines (in spite of food sufficiency), during the British Regime in India, was forceful commercialization (diversification) of agriculture (Bhattacharyya 1989).

Natural Endowments and Crops Produced in the Eastern and North-Eastern States

All the eastern States in India are well endowed with adequate water resources, varieties of soils and diverse climatic conditions to facilitate production of all major categories of agricultural crops – cereal and non-cereal food crops, pulses, potatoes, fibres, spices, plantation crops, oil seeds, fruits, vegetable etc. However, depending on the demand conditions (which depends a good deal on food habits of the population in subsistence agriculture), and modes and methods of production, the major and overwhelmingly dominating crop in this region is rice (paddy). The existing cropping-patterns of the 11 eastern States are shown below (website-1).

Arunachal Pradesh

The agriculture of the State is characterized by hilly tracts and prevalence of Jhum cultivation.

Crops Produced: Cereals: Paddy, millet, maize; Fruits: Pineapple, orange, lemon, lichee, papaya, banana, peach, walnut, almond; Vegetables: Sweet potatoes, brinjal, pumpkin, cucumber; Spices: Ginger, chillies.

Assam

The State is characterized by existence of hilly tracts and alluvial valley, humid climate with hot and cold seasons and profuse rainfall – Jhum cultivation is still prevalent in some areas.

Crops Produced: Cereals: Paddy; Fibres: Jute, cotton; Plantations: Tea, cocoanut; Various Pulses and Oilseeds, potatoes, sugarcane; Fruits: Orange and other citrus fruits, banana, guava, pineapple, mango; All sorts of vegetables.

Bihar

Characterized by the juxtaposition of fertile North Ganga Plain and hilly South Ganga Plain – both hot and cold seasons with heavy rainfall.

Crops Produced: Cereals: Paddy, wheat, maize, barley; Fibres: Jute; various oilseeds, pulses and sugarcane; Fruits: Mango, lichee and other fruits; All types of vegetables.

Jharkhand

The State consists mainly of the Chhotanagpur plateau.

Crops Produced: Cereals: Paddy, wheat and maize; various pulses.

Manipur

The state consists of hills and valleys with plain lands – rains of both summer and winter are helpful for cultivation.

Crops Produced: Cereals: Wheat, maize; Pulses, potato; Fruits: Pineapple, orange, apricot, lemon, mango; all varieties of vegetables.

Meghalaya

The State consists of hills and plateaus – cold weather with heavy rainfall – only 10% of land is cultivable.

Crops Produced: Cereals: Paddy; Oilseeds and sugarcane; Fruits: Pineapple, orange, banana.

Mizoram

The State is endowed with hilly tracts and scattered plains with rich alluvial soil – cold and humid climate.

Crops Produced: Cereals: Paddy, maize; Spices: Ginger, turmeric, chillies, pepper, cinnamon, large cardamom; Plantations: tea, coffee, rubber; Oilseeds: Mustard, sesame; Fruits: Orange, banana, pineapple; various vegetables.

Nagaland

The State is characterized by hilly, rugged terrains with heavy rainfall, and prevalence of Jhum and terraced farming.

Crops Produced: Cereals: Paddy (in 85% of cultivable land), millet, maize

Plantations: Tea, coffee; different vegetables, pulses, oilseeds, sugarcane, spices and potato.

Orissa

The State contains coastal plains, mountainous regions, plateaus, rolling uplands and sub-montane region – hot summer and cold winter with adequate rainfall. With wide variation in climate and topography almost all varieties of crops are grown in the 31 agricultural zones of the State.

Crops Produced: Cereals: Paddy, maize, millet; Plantations: Tea, coffee, rubber, cocoanut; Fibres: Jute, cotton, mesta; various oilseeds and pulses, different vegetables; Ground nut and cashew nut; Sugarcane, tobacco and various fruits.

Tripura

The State consists of hills, dales and valleys with rich alluvial soil – hot and humid climate with adequate rainfall – with vast forest coverage, only 25% land area is cultivable.

Crops Produced: Cereals: Paddy, wheat; Jute, sugarcane, cocoanut and oilseeds

West Bengal

So far as agriculture is concerned, it is the most richly endowed State in the eastern zone. With vast fertile plains, adequate rainfall, wide variations in climate, soil and topography, the State is suitable for cultivation of all varieties of crops produced in the other States in the region. But still now the dominant crop is rice (paddy).

For all the 11 States of the eastern zone taken as a whole, paddy is the dominant crop, and methods of production are still based on traditional technologies. Excepting West Bengal, there has been very little application of modern technologies. On the other hand, natural endowments are conducive to production of all varieties of crops in the region. So, there is wide scope for diversification of crops in all the four senses. Now, let us have a glimpse of the progress of crop diversification in the two major States of the region, viz. Bihar and West Bengal.

Progress of Crop Diversification in Bihar and West Bengal

Bihar

Change in cropping pattern of Bihar during the 1981- 1999 is shown in the following table.

Table-1: Change in Cropping Pattern in Bihar (in %)

S.No	Crop	1999	1981
1	Rice	44.37	45.11
2	Wheat	24.82	19.85
3	Maize	7.51	8.35
4	Barley	0.02	1.20
5	Mandua	0.03	1.10
6	Jowar	0.36	0.09
7	Gram	0.52	1.90
8	Arhar	1.16	0.74
9	Other Kharif pulses	6.68	1.24
10	Other Rabi pulses	0.73	9.04
11	Rapeseed & mustard	1.17	0.79
12	Linseed	0.63	0.99
13	Castor	0.01	0.03
14	Sesamum	0.05	0.07
15	Jute	1.79	0.38
16	Sugarcane	1.29	1.38
17	Tobacco	0.23	0.20
18	Potato	1.66	1.26
19	Onion	0.18	0.15

Source: Website-2

The table-1 above shows that a few crops like Wheat, Arhar, Other Kharif, Pulses, Rapeseed and Mustard and Jute have gained prominence in the cropping pattern in 1999-2000 over the last 2 decades, whereas a few other crops like Rabi pulses, Mandua, Barley, Linseed have been marginalized in the cropping pattern. This also reveals a tendency of persistence in cropping pattern with the share of food grains still predominant in the cropping pattern.

West Bengal

Among the Eastern States, there have been most persistent efforts towards crop diversification in West Bengal in recent years. The outcome of these efforts is shown in the following table.

Table-2: Annual Average Rate of Change in Area (%)

Food and Non-Food Crops	Between 1999 – 2003	Fruits, Flowers and Spices	Between 2002- 03 and 2003-04
Rice	– 1. 67	Fruits	5.71
Wheat	3.77	Flowers	24.93
Total Cereals	– 1.40	Spices	3.00
Pulses	4.31		
Total Food Grains	– 1.22		
Oilseeds	4.38		
Potato	3.53		
Jute	1.20		

Compiled from: Economic Review, Govt. of W. B., 2004-05, PP.18-19, 24

From table-2, it is seen that in recent years in West Bengal, there has been a shift of area against rice, in favor of wheat, pulses, oilseeds, potato, jute, fruits, flowers and spices.

With persistent efforts of the Government of West Bengal, the process of diversification has been accelerated. At present the following policies have been adopted by the Department of Agriculture, Government of W.B

a) Increase land under horticulture.

b) Introduction of new varieties of crop diversification, including cultivation of pulses, oilseeds and tobacco.

c) Draw up block wise horticulture production plan (Website-3).

The policies of the government of W.B. emphasizing rapid crop diversification, especially, in favor of horticulture, floriculture and other "high-valued" crops may, in course of time, be imitated by all other States in the eastern region, and so far as natural conditions are concerned, this is quite feasible. But the pertinent question in this regard is the consequences of such diversification for the poor. We are going to take up this issue in the next section of our study.

Consequences for the Poor

Crop diversification in the eastern zone, according to present policy, has two major thrust areas:

i) From cereals to oilseeds and pulses, and

ii) From conventional crops to so-called 'high-valued' crops, especially horticulture and floriculture.

So far as the first aspect is concerned there is sufficient domestic excess demand to justify increase in production of oilseeds and pulses through increase in area and productivity (by transition from traditional to modern technologies).

As regards the second aspect, sustainability depends mainly on expanding foreign market. In this area agro-processing is an urgent necessity (assuming that all the expectations about rapidly expanding export market would be realized). In this area supply side calls for heavy investment for both production and processing. The latter also calls for technological up gradation with foreign technologies in most of the cases. Thus it is evident that diversification in this sense would emphasize the role of the big players including domestic large industrial houses as well as giant MNCs from the developed countries. The various policy announcements as given below substantiate this view.

I: In the Global Convention Food - World India 2005, organised by FICCI, the Chief Minister of West Bengal, Mr. Buddhadeb Bhattacharjee said, "Frito Lays of Pepsi and Dabur (in pineapple processing) are already in the state. Metro Group of Germany has met me several times and we are going to finalise their project soon whereby they will set up a food chain and will also supply to all the hotels in and around Kolkata as they have almost finalised their program". He informed that besides Germany, countries like France, Italy and Japan have been taking interest in entering the food sector in west Bengal.

W.B. has created six Agro-Export Zones for pineapple, lichee, mango, potato, vegetables and cashew nuts for developing an internationally competitive production base for a particular produce. Some of the leading investors in the food sector in W.B. are Pepsi Co. (through Frito Lays India); Dabur; Nestle; Venkateshwara Hatcheries; Potato King Pvt. Ltd; Elque & Co. and Keventor Bio Tech. Calypso is likely to begin its production soon in West Bengal (Website-4).

II: In the inaugural address in the Conference for Greater Growth & Market Action in Food Processing in Bihar, Jharkhand, Orissa and West Bengal held at New Delhi in January 30, 2006, Sri Buddhadeb Bhattacharjee, the Chief Minister of west Bengal, appreciated FICCI's role in promoting and developing the food processing industry. "FICCI has taken much initiative, and it should now form a cell to see how the private sector can create facilities like cold chain infrastructure," he suggested.

"The real problem for us (in West Bengal) is the lack of a marketing mechanism," Shri Bhattacharjee said, noting that even while being the largest producer of vegetables and several varieties of fruits, sometimes as much as 30% of the produce perished. "We have five food parks and five export zones, but we must have public-private collaboration to create infrastructure facilities."

In his special address at the seminar "Focus East - Promoting Food Processing in Bihar, Jharkhand, Orissa and West Bengal," the Union Minister of Food Processing Industries, Shri Subodh Kant Sahai lauded FICCI's efforts in this area, and suggested it to set up a special cell in FICCI to map the eastern states and draw up a road map. Sri Sahai said that the country should strive to increase its share of value addition in agricultural and processed products from 6% to 20% and eventually to 30%. The global export share would also go up from 1% to 3%. He, however, emphasized that exports could not grow without development of the wholesale sector.

In his welcome address, FICCI's eastern region council chairman Shri C.K. Dhanuka said that while the four eastern states together contributed approximately 20% of India's agricultural output, much of it remained untapped. "The eastern region can become a critical link in the global food value chain," he added. Shri Dhanuka also suggested a series of measures for the state governments to adopt, including providing incentives to promote public-private partnerships in the food processing sector, and creation of state-specific plans to attract both domestic and foreign investment (website-5).

In fact, the policies related to diversification of agriculture in India have opened up the opportunities for entry of the giant MNCs into the Indian market. Some of the giant MNCs taking entry into the Indian agricultural market are: Agre Evo (ProAgro), Aventis, Bayer Crop, Bejo Zaden, Cargill, Cyanamid, Dow, Hicks Muse Fuse Trust, Hoechst, Monsanto, Nickersen Zwaan, Novartis, Nunhems, Pioneer, Royal Sluis, Sun, Syngenta, Zeneca.

It is doubt if this process is going to benefit the poor.

References

Bhattacharyya, Dhires (1989): A Concise history of Indian Economy, Prentice-Hall of India Pvt. Ltd., New Delhi

Government of West Bengal: Economic Review, various issues

Kangle, R. P. (1986): Kautīlya Arthaśāstra, Part-II [English translation], Motilal Banarasidass, Delhi. [In quotations, II/24/1 means Book-II, Chapter-24, Śloka-1 etc.]

Website-1: [http://www.webindia123.com/states/index.htm]

Website-2: [http://patna.bih.nic.in/html/croppingpatternofbihar.htm]

Website-3: [http://64.233.179.104/search?q=cache:sPVjYlJTe8oJ:agricoop.nic.in/Kharif2006/Kharif2006ppt/west%2520Bengal.ppt+department+of+agriculture,+govt.+of+west+be

Website-4:

[http://64.233.179.104/search?q=cache:ryG4bsMHWvIJ:www.ficci.com/ficciimage/88888888_1134/west-begal.doc+food+processing+industries+in+west+bengal&hl=en&

Website-5:

[http://www.ficci.com/ficci/media-room/speeches-presentations/2006/jan/30jan-food-kol-press.htm]

Chapter 2. Ancient India's Foreign Trade with East Asia

Introduction

The economic, cultural and political relation between India and East Asia, which developed through trade relations, may be traced back to the pre-historic age. This relation continued through the historic period and assumed new dimensions. Till the Christian era evidence of such trade are derived from discovery of Indian articles and use of Indian names in distant lands and mention of India's trade with Suvarnabhumī, Suvarnadvīpa, Javadvīpa, Tāmradvīpa etc. in Buddhist Jātakas, Rāmāyana, Mahābhārata, Purānas etc. Ancient Tamil poems mentioned ports like Barukachchha, Rovurā, Kāviri-Pattinum etc.

During the Christian era, while Indians had to face powerful competition from Arab and Roman merchants in the West, the field practically lay open to them in the East. In the latter half of the first century A.D., the spirit of maritime adventure of India found its full scope in the South-East – Indonesia, Indo-China and Malaya Archipelago.

During the Gupta Era, there was a regular trade relation between Tāmralipti and Ceylon, Indonesia and Indo-China. During the third decade of the sixth century A.D., there developed an inter-coastal trade route linking east coast of India with Ceylon, Indonesia and China. Since the 8th century A.D., India's trade with East and South-East Asia started declining and in course of the next 300 years it became almost insignificant.

Pre-Christian Era

The sources of information for this period are very scanty. Most of the information are derived from archaeological evidence, and at times, inductions. Sometimes, we are to rely upon indirect evidence such as the discovery of Indian articles in distant lands or the use of Indian names for those articles.

Philological researches have established a connection between the Neolithic peoples of India and the primitive tribes that inhabited Indo-china, Malaya Peninsula and Indonesian islands. The German scholar Schmitz, e.g., holds that the languages of many Indian tribes belong to the same family of speech (called Austric) from which those of the peoples of Indo-china and Indonesia have been derived (Majumdar, Roychoudhury & Datta, 1980, PP. 14-15).

It may be presumed that from time immemorial the people of India had free and intimate intercourse with the outside world. Even in the dim pre-historic age, Neolithic people, as already mentioned, had relations with the Far East and there are good reasons to believe that they emigrated from India by large numbers, both by land and by sea, and got settled in Indo-China and Indonesian islands. In the succeeding age, while an advanced civilization flourished in the Indus Valley, there was undoubtedly a familiar intercourse with the countries by which India was surrounded on the north, east and west and the relation continued through the historic period (Ibid. P. 202).

There are mentions of India's trade with Suvarnabhumī, Suvarnadvīpa, Javadvīpa, Tāmradvīpa etc. in Jātakas & other Buddhist texts, Rāmāyana, Mahābhārata, Purānas, Kathāsarit Sāgara, Haribhamsa, Rāmāyana Manjarī of Kshemendra, Mahābhāsya of Patanjali etc. (Smith, V., 1974, PP. 185-188; Ghosal, U. N., 1957, P. 447). There are evidence of India's foreign trade in ancient Tamil poems, which mention the names of ancient ports like Barukachchha, Rovurā, Kāviri-Pattinum (the capital of the Cholas), Champā (modern Bhagalpur) etc. (Rhys Davis, 1962, PP. 189-190).

Buddhism was an important factor in developing India's trade relations with East Asia during this period. Buddhism, chiefly in its Mahājāna form, along with many aspects of Indian culture and tradition, was carried by courageous monks to the lands beyond the sea. It is highly significant that the earliest material evidence of contact between India and South-East Asia takes the form of Buddhist images (of the school of Amarāvati) which have been found in Thailand, Kampuchea, Sumatra and Java (Smith, op. cit. PP. 185-188).

The nature of the imports and exports are seldom specified. Gems of various kinds, muslins, the finer sorts of cloth, cutlery, armor, brocades, embroideries, rugs, perfumes, drugs, ivory works, gold, jewelry etc., were the main articles of trade (Majumdar, Roychoudhury & Datta, 1980, PP. 205-06).

Early Christian Era

While Indian traders had to face competition from powerful Arab and Roman merchants in the West, they were free from such hindrances in the East. Chinese writers mentioned that very large ships used to sail from the Chola ports in the latter half of the first century A.D. They also recorded the voyages of Indian merchants to Malaya and Cambodia in the third century A.D. Takkola, Tamalin, Javadvīpa, Suvarnakūta and Suvarnabhūmi are included among the places across the high seas visited by the Indian merchants. Ptolemy mentioned, as the places visited by Indian merchants, Golden Chersonese (Malaya Peninsula) and also described the island of Iabidios, i.e., the island of barley, as producing much gold and silver. Its capital, according to him, was called Argyre, i.e., the silver town. Contemporary and subsequent Greek, Indian and Arab writing testify that it was mainly the quest of gold that drew the Indian merchants across the sea to Indo-China and Indonesia (Ghosal, 1957, PP. 446-447).

The spirit of maritime adventure of India found its scope in the South-East. Across the Bay of Bengal, lay Indo-china and Malaya Archipelago. The Eastern Coast of India from the mouth of the Ganges to Cape Comorin (Kanyā Kumāri) was studded with ports. Some of these ports are mentioned in the famous book "Periplus of the Erethrean Sea". The author refers to some of the far eastern countries as Chryse, i.e., the golden land. From the descriptions of this book, it could be inferred that there was a coasting voyage from Bengal to these regions. Ptolemy, who wrote in the 2nd century A.D., knew the names of important trading centers in Malaya Peninsula, and the islands of Java and Sumatra. Buddhist texts, written about the same period, give a long list of trading centers in the Far East, which agree fairly well with that of Ptolemy. These names are mostly in Sanskrit. Thus, by the 2nd century A.D., the Indians had developed important trade relations with the Far East. We learn from Ptolemy that there was a direct trade route from Palura (near Ganjam district of Orissa) across the sea to the Malaya Peninsula (Majumdar, Roychoudhuri & Datta, 1980, PP. 205-06).

Gupta Era (240-495 A.D.)

During the Gupta Era, there was all round prosperity of India and as a part of this, foreign trade also flourished. During this period Ceylon used to enjoy a central position for trade purposes. The ports of East and West Coasts of India were linked together through Ceylon. There was a regular commercial connection between Tāmralipti (modern Tamluk in West Bengal) and Ceylon on the one hand, and Indonesia and Indo-China on the other (Mahajan, 1986, P. 467).

During this period ships plied between ports on Bay of Bengal and other Asian countries. Besides Tāmralipti, the people of Kalinga and the Tamil states had also a great share in this traffic. There was also a regular commercial connection between the Eastern Coast of India and West Asia, Africa and Europe. The Chinese pilgrim Fa-hien, who came to India during the 5th century A.D., sailed from Tāmralipti to Java via Ceylon, and again from Java to China in Indian ship.

Commodities traded, according to Cosmas in his Christian Topography written in 547 A.D. included spices (cinnamon, long pepper, white pepper, cardamom), spikenards, aromatics, fragrant trees, sesame logs, medicinal plants, sandalwood, asaphoetida, aloes, cloves, corals, pearls, raw silk, silk yarn, silk robes, ivory, musk, various textile products etc. (Majumdar, 1960, P. 455).

In fact, it is very difficult to distinguish exports from imports because, very often, the commodities imported into India from some countries were re-exported to other countries.

Post Gupta Era

The most important event in the history of Eastern and Southern Asia during this period was the development, by the 3rd decade of the 6th century, of an inter oceanic trade reaching from China through Indonesia and East Coast of India up to Ceylon, and extending there along the West Indian Coast to Persia, Arabia and Ethiopia. According to Cosmas, merchandise from China, Indonesia and South India were carried to Ceylon. Whence it was exported the Western Lands just mentioned and India had a fair share in this inter oceanic trade that linked East Asia with West Asia, Africa and Europe.

Ceylon used to play the intermediary role as it was much frequented by ships from all parts of India and East Asia on the one hand and from Persia, Ethiopia and other western lands on the other. The Chinese Buddhist pilgrims from Fa-hien downwards on their return journeys or both used the sea route from Tāmralipti. Besides these overseas routes, a number of overland routes connected India and China (Majumdar, 1962, PP. 598-600).

The articles imported from South-East Asia were mainly silk, camphor, bees' wax, cloves, sandalwood and cardamom. Spices were imported from Java and Sumatra. Chinese silk was also imported from this region. India used to import pearls, dry-ginger and tin from Ceylon. During this period Tāmralipti was still the most important port of Bengal. The other important ports on the Eastern Coast were: Puri, Chiccaculi, Banpur, and Ramesvara. Important ports on the Western Coast were: Quilon, Mangalore, Thana, Sopara, Kambay, Sindan, Debal and Bhrigukachchha.

From the beginning of the 8th century A.D., the Arabs became the most dominant maritime power and Indian foreign trade to the West Asia, Africa and Rome were lost to them. The Arab and Chinese competition gradually led to shrinkage of India's foreign trade with East and South-East Asia also and, in course of the next 300 years, it became almost insignificant. The decline of trade led to the decay of many towns and ports, e.g., Purāna Quilā (Delhi), Kausambī (near Allahabad), Mathurā, Hastināpur (Meerut district), Rājghāt (Varanasi), Chirand (Saran district), Vaiśālī etc. On account of the restricted market for Indian exports, artisans and merchants living in those towns and ports shifted to the countryside and took to cultivation (Mahajan, 1986, PP. 672-674).

Hindu Kingdoms in East Asia

As a follow up of trade various Hindu kingdoms emerged in East Asia. To avoid misgivings, it should be pointed out that the term Hindu here is not referred to a specific religious group known by the same term, but in a wider sense to mean the philosophy and culture of ancient Hindustan that includes India, Bangladesh, Pakistan and parts of Afghanistan. In ancient times all people (whether Brahminical, Jainists or Buddhists) from Hindustan were known in East, West and South Asia as Hindus. The kingdoms I am going to mention here were mainly associated with Buddhist and Brahminical religious groups. From pre-historic times Hindustan had developed wide trade relations with all the East Asian countries and there was continuous flow of people, culture and religious ideas from Hindustan to these countries and in the process, several Hindu kingdoms sprang up in various parts of East Asia.

Champā (Vietnam)

Hindu kingdoms were established in Champā, the eastern coast of Indo-China, now known as Annam. Bhadra Vareman, one of the early kings, ruled nearly over the whole of modern Annam (excluding Tonkin and Cochin-China), divided into three provinces known as Amarāvatī, Vijaya and Pānduranga. Tonkin, the country immediately to the north, was peopled by Annamites, and formed a part of the Chinese Empire. The Hindu kings of Champā, anxious to extend their powers northwards, often came into conflict with the Chinese Empire and suffered invasions by the imperial troops, sometimes with disastrous consequences. Lateron, Annamites becoming independent and they were in constant hostilities with Champā.

Major kings of different dynasties were: Śambhu Varman, Satya Varman, Indra Varman, Hari Varman, Simha Varman etc. In 1190 A. D., Jaya Varman VII, the king of Kambuja, defeated Jaya-Indra Varman of Champā, took him captive and annexed Champā. Thereafter Champā regained independence after 30 year's war, but in 1282, suffered great defeat by the Mongal Chief, Kubla Khan. Annamites gradually conquered Champā by the end of 15th century A.D. (Majumdar, 1960, P. 479)

Kambuja (Cambodia)

According to Chinese chronicles, Fu-nan, the earliest Hindu kingdom in East Asia, was founded by the Brahmin, Kaundinya before the third century A.D. He was the first Emperor in Indo-China. Jaya Varman and Rudra Varman of the dynasty ruled during the sixth century.

Early in the seventh century, Kambuja, originally a vassal state of Fu-nan, conquered Fu-nan, became the leading power in the region and gave the name to the whole country. In the eighth century, the Sailendra king of Java conquered Kambuja, but it gained independence under Jaya Varman II who ruled from 802 to 854. The most powerful king after him was Yasa Varman who ruled from 889 to 908. The dynasty ruled till 1001 with political authority over Siam, Laos and probably Yunnan,.

Surya Varman, founder of the next dynasty, established authority over northern Siam and invaded lower Burma. Surya Varman II, who constructed the famous Ankar Vat temple, ruled from 1113 to 1150. Jaya Varman VII, who ascended throne in 1181, made Champā a vassal state of Kambuja and conquered portions of lower Burma.

The kingdom declined during the 13th century because of Thai invasion (Ibid. PP. 480-481).

Brahmadeśa (Myanmar)

The Hinduised Mon settlements in lower Burma were known collectively as Ramannadeśa. They had a powerful kingdom in the seventh century A.D. To the north of the Mons, the Hinduised Pyus established a kingdom with Śrīkshetra as the capital. The Pyus occupied the Irawadi valley as early as the third century A.D. and continued as a great political power till the ninth century.

The Hinduised Mrammas poured into Burma in large numbers in the ninth and tenth centuries and founded an independent kingdom with Pagan as capital. Their first king Aniruddha ruled from 1044 to 1077 and was succeeded by two sons. The dynasty ruled till 1287. Thereafter, the Mongals occupied their kingdom. But Indian culture and tradition still persists in Myanmar (Ibid. PP. 484-488).

Java

According to Chinese chronicles, there were two Hindu kingdoms in the island of Java in the fifth century A. D. – Cho-po and Ho-lo-tan. Title of the kings of both these kingdoms was Varman.

Four Sanskrit inscriptions by the king Purna Varman has been found in Batavia. He ruled western Java during 6th century A.D. His capital was Taruma. He dug a vast canal and named it Gomatī River. Earlier his father Rājādhirāja had dug a similar canal and named it Chandrabhāgā River.

Chinese works of the Sui period (589-906 A.D.) give evidence of the existence of several Hindu kingdoms and 28 feudatory Hindu kings in the island of Java during the subsequent period. During the Tang period, the kingdom of Ho-ling emerged in central Java. The name of the kingdom suggests that it had close relation with Kalinga , i.e. modern Orissa (Majumdar, 1962, PP. 651).

The Sailendra kings ruled Java since the 8th century A.D. They became extremely powerful and conquered Sumatra and many other kingdoms of East Asia. The famous Barabudur temple was constructed by these kings. Later on the kingdom became weak and fell after the Chola attack in the 11th century.

During the 14th century, the Majapahit kings emerged in Java and brought under their control most of Indonesia and Malaya. The history of the Hindu kingdoms in Java ended after the onslaught of Islam in the 15th century A.D. (Smith, 1974, PP. 185-188).

Sumatra

The earliest Hindu kingdom in the island of Sumatra was established in Sri-Vijaya in the 4th century A.D. Malaya was brought under its control. Since 684 Sri-Vijaya was ruled by the Buddhist king Jayanāga who conquered Java in 686. According to the Chinese author I-tsing, Sri-vijaya was a great centre of Buddhist learning and culture. Inscriptions discovered at Ligor in Malaya peninsula describe the vast naval and commercial power of the kingdom of Sri-Vijaya, which could successfully carry on its aggressive policy during the 8th century, but later on was conquered by the Sailendras of Java (Majumdar, 1962, PP. 650-651).

Borneo

The Hindu colonization of eastern Borneo is substantiated by seven Sanskrit inscriptions found at Muara Kaman, an important sea-port in ancient times. These inscriptions refer to the king Mūla Varman and his grandson Kundungo. The inscriptions give testimony to the great predominance of the Brahmins and Hindu culture in the island of Borneo.

The Hindu colonies advanced into the interior of eastern Borneo along Mahākām River. Similarly, the discoveries of archaeological remains on the banks of Kapuas River show that the Hindus colonized western Borneo and set up a number of settlements in the valley of this river. (Ibid. PP. 652-653)

Bali

The Hindus had colonized the island of Bali and set up a kingdom there before 6th century A.D. The Chinese history of Leang dynasty (502-557 A.D.) gives the following interesting account of Bali: "The king's family name is Kaudinya and he said that the wife of Suddhadana was a daughter of his country."

In 518 A.D. the king of Bali sent an envoy to China. The name Kaundinya is interesting and shows the influence of that family in all the Hindu colonies of Suvarnadvīpa (Indonesia). The Chinese author gives a detailed account of the manners and splendors of the Royal Court, which testifies to the fact that in the 6th century A.D. the island of Bali was the seat of a prosperous Hindu kingdom. (Ibid. P. 653)

After the onslaught of Islam during the 15th century A.D., the Hindu cultural influence subsided in most of the Indonesian islands except Bali. The remnants of Hindu culture and tradition in Indonesia still linger in the island of Bali.

References

Ghosal, Dr. U. N. (1957): "Economic Conditions (Post Mauryan)", in K. A. Nilakanta Sastri (ed.): A Comprehensive History of India, Vol. II, the Mauryas and Satvahanas, Ch. XXIV, PP. 430-457, Orient Longmans, Bombay, Calcutta, Madras

Mahajan, Vidya Dhar (1986): Ancient India, S. Chand & Co. Pvt. Ltd., New Delhi

Majumdar, R. C. (1960): Ancient India, Motilal Banarasi Dass, Delhi

Majumdar, R.C. (ed.) (1962): The History and Culture of the Indian People, the Classical Age, Ch. XXIV, Bharatiya Vidya Bhavan

Majumdar, R. C., Roychoudhury, H. C., & Datta, Kalikinkar (1980): An Advanced History of India, Macmillan Company of India, Madras

Rhys Davis, Mrs. C. A. F. (1962): "Economic Conditions According to Early Buddhist Literature", in E. J. Rapson (ed.): The Cambridge History of India, Vol. I. Ancient India, Ch. VIII, S. Chand & Co., Delhi (Second Indian Reprint)

Smith, Vincent A. (1974): The Oxford History of India, Oxford University Press, Delhi

Chapter 3. Ethical Basis of Exploitation of the Dalits in India

Introduction

The most intricate issue pertaining to deprivation, discrimination, exploitation and oppression in India since independence is the dalit issue.

The term "dalit" means downtrodden and trampled. In fact the dalits in India, the lowest of the lower castes and the poorest of the poor, are being trampled (socially, politically and economically) by the rich, especially those belonging to the upper castes.

It is very difficult to estimate exactly the number of dalits in India. But the most liberal estimate would make the number larger than the population of most of the countries of the world except China, India, USA and Indonesia. Roughly they comprise about 16.48 per cent of India's population. But their share of ownership of land and property, and access to education and employment and basic social amenities is miserably lower. The worst inhuman practice against them is the practice of untouchability, which is rampant in all the states of India. This is associated with various kinds of atrocities perpetrated on them by the rich (mostly belonging to the upper castes and the upper strata of the lower castes). All these social exploitation have been associated with economic exploitation and slavery.

Most of the evidences reveal that the administrative machineries of all the State governments have been playing a negative and pro-rich role in all cases of exploitation, atrocities and oppression of dalits by the upper castes and the rich irrespective of caste, although there are some legal provisions to prevent such activities to some extent.

All policies like land reforms and other measures intended to empower the dalits (economically, socially or politically) have been foiled by the bureaucrats belonging to the upper castes and the privileged minority (through the policy of reservation) of the lower castes.

So far as the motivation of the policies of the government is concerned, it has been to isolate the advanced segment of the dalits and lower castes from the downtrodden majority, and to create a lower caste aristocracy to distract attention from the basic problems of the exploited majority. Moreover, the method of reservation has given a permanent stamp of social inferiority to all lower castes including the dalits. So the short-term job or other opportunities offered to the advanced minority has long term adverse consequences for the majority as the legal recognition of caste distinctions would be very difficult to erase even if the majority of the dalits were economically and politically empowered unless they change their surnames after being empowered.

So in all respects the dalits in India reveal a miserable picture and an affront to humanity. Their plight has further degenerated in course of economic reforms since 1991 because of endangerment of food security, shrinkage of employment opportunities, inflation, reduction of social sector amenities and increasing incidence of violence and atrocities by the upper castes.

In this paper, however, we are not going to explore these matters in detail. [For detail see Website: 1-13]. Our task here is to trace the origin of the concept and exploitation of the dalits in India and to highlight the ethical aspects of this issue. Our main purpose here is to point out that the dalits could never be empowered in the true sense of the term unless we change our values and attitudes, the inherent unethical psychosis of building up our economic, political and social positions at the cost of the majority of the human race.

In general, the root of the malady may be traced back to Manusmriti (M.S.) and its basic psychic origin. The M.S., as available today, reveals a great departure from the professed norms of caste system on the basis of qualities (not on heredity) and to serve the purpose of division of labour. In fact, practice of caste system in its real form always revealed a design of the well to do minority to live on the surplus generated by the majority. So it actually became hereditary and became the most powerful tool of economic exploitation, which brought as necessary concomitants social and political aspects of the caste system. M.S. only ascribed a legal, ethical and religious justification to the existing system of exploitation. M.S. delineated how plethora of new sub-castes was generated by inter-caste marriage and thus the forefathers of the modern dalits emerged. We are going to look into these aspects in this article.

Plight of the Dalits in India Today

The dalits, belonging mainly to the lowest castes and comprising about 16.48 per cent of India's population, are mainly landless agricultural labourers and they are the poorest and the most vulnerable section of Indian society. [Website-1]

According to some surveys, 48 per cent of the dalits live below the poverty line, 70 per cent are landless or near landless, and the rate of illiteracy stands at 63 per cent. [Website-11]

It has been estimated that in the rural sector more than 75 per cent of the dalit workers arc still connected with agriculture and allied activities – 50 percent landless labourers and the rest (25 per cent) marginal and small farmers. Urban dalits work mainly in the unorganized sector. Only 1.1 million (0.8%), out of the total dalit population of 138 million, have been benefited by the policy of reservation. [Website-4]

Majority of the bonded labourers in India are dalits. According to official statistics, about one million dalits are manual scavengers who clear feces from public and private latrines and dispose of dead animals. Unofficial estimates are much higher. In South India, dalit girls are forced into prostitution before reaching the age of puberty. These girls are dedicated to prostitution in the name of devadasis, literally meaning "female servants of god". They are not permitted to marry and ultimately, they are sold to urban brothels. [Website-13]

Rape of dalit girls is a common crime in rural India and the upper caste people do not follow the rules of untouchability in this case.

Sometimes this serves the upper castes in two ways – fulfillment of perverted desires and punishment for protests or attempts to exercise political rights by dalit women. [Ibid]

The worst deprivation and exploitation of the dalits come in the form of untouchability. In fact, it has been for a very long time an extremely sophisticated economic and political strategy to ensure cheap and slave labour so as to live on the surplus product of the majority by the well-to-do minority. [Website-1]

Untouchability is the basis for denial of basic needs, land rights and civil liberties, legal discrimination, inferior status, sub-human living and working conditions, mal-nourishment, bad health conditions, high levels of illiteracy, atrocities and violence. [Website-13]

Untouchability was abolished under Article 17 of the Indian constitution. But still the practice continues to determine the socio-economic and religious standing of the dalits. Dalits are not generally permitted to change the occupational structures into which they are born. [Ibid]

In most of the States in India, dalits are forced to live in segregated slums on the outskirts of villages and the location of the slums is determined by economic factors, viz. the requirement of free or cheap labour, with some pseudo religious justification. Some of the examples of this heinous crime against humanity are given below. [Website-1]

1. In many villages of the country, the dalit postmen are not permitted to cycle through the upper caste sections and if they violate this edict, they are severely beaten up and do not get any protection of existing laws against such violence.

2. In many areas teashops keep separate glasses for the dalits.

3. Dalits are beaten up for dressing better and are not permitted, in the Hindi belt, to mount a horse in a barat (bridegroom's party), which is a conventional custom for the upper castes.

4. Various underhand methods are adopted by the upper castes to deprive the dalits of their democratic right of voting.

5. Dalits have been deprived of their rights over common properties through privatization of these properties.

6. Untouchability is also to be found in many educational institutions in most of the States.

7. Dalits are not permitted to enter the temples in many areas.

8. In many areas even high level dalit employees find it difficult to hire a rented house unless they change their surnames.

9. The caste system and segregation of the dalits is not only confined to the Hindu community, but also it is practiced by the Christians and Muslims.

The reform measures have led to aggravation of the conditions of the dalits in India in all respects because of the following reasons. [Website-4]

a) Food Security: Food security of the dalits has been endangered because of

i) reduction of subsidies on fertilizers, ii) increasing exports and free market sales of food-grains leading to a drastic reduction in the stocks of food-grains with the public procurement agencies, ii) the reforms in banking with a severe squeeze on agriculture lending leading to fall in food-grains production, iv) the promising income from wheat export resulting in substitution of coarse cereals, the main food of the dalits, in many areas, v) PDS prices, owing to reduction of food-subsidies, becoming unaffordable by the dalits.

b) Inflation: Rapid inflation, caused by reform policies [reduction in the budget and fiscal deficit, devaluation, privatization, elimination or reduction of subsidies and export promotion], has raised the prices of most of the essential consumption goods of the dalits leading to further deterioration of their conditions.

c) Employment: Reform policies have led to drastic fall in the rate of growth of employment opportunities in both the organized and the unorganized sectors. The worst victims of this trend have been the dalits. Along with this, the cut in government expenditure on various poverty alleviation programs has enhanced the incidence of abject poverty of the dalits.

From the above analysis it appears that empowerment of the dalits in India is an urgent necessity. But the question is how to devise a appropriate means to accomplish this Herculean task. To device a correct policy, it is necessary to go into the origin of this inhuman exploitation of the dalits and analyze its economic and psychic basis. The explicit origin of this practice may be traced back to the ancient Indian sacred text Manusmriti. So let us first have a glimpse of the prescriptions in this text regarding caste system and caste-based discrimination.

Caste System in India

The existing caste structure in India has a long history of evolution and its roots may be traced back in the Purusha Sukta of the Rig Veda, the most ancient religious and philosophical treatise of India. Now let us first have a glance at the original caste division as conceived by the ancient Indian shastras (religious, philosophical and legal texts of ancient India).

The four major castes, (i.e. hierarchical ranking of the society) in India prescribed first in the Rig Veda and repeated and elaborated in later shastras were:

1. Brahmana: Priests and scholars engaged in religious, academic, literary and philosophical activities.

2. Kshatriya: Political rulers, warriors and soldiers.

3. Vaishya: Persons engaged in trade, commerce and productive activities.

4. Shudra: The lowest caste in the Aryan hierarchy, comprising the majority of the population and serving the three upper classes. They were mainly laborers, peasants, artisans, and servants of the three upper classes.

The ancient Indian term for caste was 'varna' i.e. complexion. In general people belonging to the three upper castes were of fair complexion and the Shudras of swarthy complexion. So, it may be conceived that the former were were primarily Aryans (believed to be belonging to Cacasoid whilte races from central Asia which had invaded India and subjugated the ingenous people and got settled as rulers of the Indian suncontinent) and the Shudras, indigenous people (mainly proto-Australoid or Dravida) whom the Aryans had subjugated while invading the Indian subcontinent and incorporated these vanquished black people into the Aryan hierarchy as the fourth and serving class for their own interest.

The Vedic Concept

The relevant sloka from Rig Veda is:

"The Brahmanas were His Mouth, the Kshatriyas became His Arms, The Vaishyas were His Thighs, and the Shudras were assigned to His Feet" (Rig Veda, 10.90.12)3.

Caste System in Manusmriti

Manu opines that the creator has assigned specific duties to specific classes of people and to substantiate his views he repeats the Vedic concept viz., Brahmins originated from the mouth, Kshatriyas from the arms, Vaishyas from the thighs, and Shudras from the feet of the creator. So, they have different functions in all the ages. To quote:

1.87. But in order to protect this universe He, the most resplendent one, assigned separate duties and occupations to those who sprang from his mouth, arms, thighs, and feet4.

10.5. In all castes those children only which are begotten in the direct order on wedded wives, equal in castes and married as virgins, are to be considered as belonging to the same caste as their fathers5.

The lowest caste, viz. the Shudras, forming the majority of the population, was turned into almost slaves of the minority upper three through the guideline that the primary function of the Shudras is to serve the three upper castes. To quote:

1/91: One occupation only the lord prescribed to the Shudra, to serve meekly even these other three castes6.

Manu opines that if a person belonging to any caste relinquishes his assigned duties and adopts some forbidden duty, he will be degenerated, unless he is compelled to do so by unavoidable pressure of circumstances. To quote:

12.70: But men of the four castes, who have relinquished without the pressure of necessity their proper occupation, will become the servants of Dasyus, after migrating into despicable bodies7.

It appears that Manu emphasized that division of labour according to castes should be based on heredity.

Caste System in Mahabharata

From certain slokas of the epic Mahabharata, it may appear at first sight that the epic insisted on determination of caste of a person by his propensities and talents and not by birth. To quote:

"Everyone derives his own nature from the nature of his acts, in respect of their circumstances, place, and means and motives." (Ganguli, Sec-62)8.

"Men, however, are always engaged in those acts to which their propensities lead. Those propensities, again, lead a living being to every direction." (Ibid. Sec-62)9.

A deeper look would, however, make it clear that the above statements were relevant only to jatis, .i.e. the sub-castes within the four major castes based on specific occupation or type of activity, but not to the four major castes. It may be conceived that there was no restriction on free movement among the sub-castes but this was movements among the four major castes were strictly prohibited. The following sloka may throw further light on the matter:

"Agriculture, rearing of cattle, trade and other acts of a similar nature, should be caused to be carried on by many persons on the principle of division of labour." (Ibid. Sec-88-p.200)10.

The epic insists that economic activities like agriculture, trade etc. should be conducted on the basis of division of labour. This is different from social division of labour on the basis of castes. It is the division of labour within each category of production on the basis of efficiency.

The major social division of labour prescribed in the epic is based on the basic Indian rule - division of the society into four major castes, viz. Brahmana, Kshatriya, Vaishya and Shudra and assignment of specific duties to each caste. Their duties are in brief:

"Menial service attaches to the Shudra; agriculture to the Vaishya; the science of chastisement to the Kshatriya, and Brahmacharya, penances, mantras, and truth, attach, to the Brahmana." (Ibid. Sec-91, p-206)11.

Mahabharata, however, mentions that a Brahmana by birth would be degraded if he fails to abide by the rules prescribed for his caste. To quote:

"That wretched Brahmana who falls away from his duties and whose behavior becomes wicked, becomes, O king, a Shudra. The Brahmana who weds a Shudra woman, who becomes vile in conduct or a dancer or a village servant or does other improper acts, becomes a Shudra. Whether he recites the Vedas or not, O king, if he does such improper acts, he becomes equal to a Shudra and on occasions of feeding he should be assigned a place amongst Shudras. Such Brahmanas become equal to Shudras, O king, and should be discarded on occasions of worshipping the Gods." (Ibid. Sec-63)12.

"The Brahmana who is addicted to the practices of Kshatriyas and Vaishyas and Shudras, incurs censure in this world as a person of wicked soul and goes to hell in the next world. Those names which are applied among men to slaves and dogs and wolves and (other) beasts, are applied, O son of Pandu, to the Brahmana who is engaged in pursuits that are improper for him." (Ibid. Sec-62)13.

There is, however, no rule for up gradation of a person from a lower to an upper caste.

Shudras were being exploited by the three upper castes.

Manu prescribes for prohibition of wealth accumulation by a Shudra. To quote:

10.129. No collection of wealth must be made by a Shudra, even though he be able (to do it); for a Shudra who has acquired wealth, gives pain to Brahmanas14.

Still the Shudras were part of the Aryan social hierarchy. On the other hand, the mlechchas (barbarians) and outcastes (mixed castes) from which the modern dalits have descended were not considered to be part of the Aryan social hierarchy. The origin of the outcastes has been described in detail in Manusmriti. Manu defines them as mixed castes originating from intermarriage of the four castes.

Caste System in Manusmriti

Manu opines that the creator has assigned specific duties to specific classes of people. According to Manu, Brahmins originated from the mouth, Ksatriyas from the arms, Vaiśyas from the thighs, and Śūdras from the feet of the creator. So, they have different functions in all the ages. To quote:

1/87: But in order to protect his universe He, the most resplendent one, assigned separate [duties and] occupations to those who sprang from his mouth, arms, thighs and feet.

The lowest caste, viz. the Śūdras, forming the majority of the population, was turned into almost slaves of the minority three through the guideline that the primary function of the Śūdras is to serve the three upper castes.To quote:

1/91: One occupation only the lord prescribed to the Śūdra, to serve meekly even these [other] three castes.

Manu opines that if a person belonging to any caste relinquishes their assigned duties and adopts some forbidden duty, will be degenerated, unless he is compelled to do so by unavoidable pressure of circumstances. To quote:

12/70: But men of the four castes, who have relinquished without the pressure of necessity their proper occupation, will become the servants of Dasyus, after migrating into despicable bodies.

It appears that Manu considered division of labour according to castes was hereditary. To quote:

10/5: In all castes those [children] only which are begotten in the direct order on wedded wives, equal [in castes and married as] virgins, are to be considered as belonging to the

same caste [as their fathers].

Manu also prescribes for prohibition of wealth accumulation by a Śūdra. To quote:

10/129: No collection of wealth must be made by a Śūdra, even though he be able [to do it]; for a Śūdra who has acquired wealth, gives pain to Brahmins.

Mixed Castes and Origin of the Dalits

Besides the four major castes many mixed-castes originated because of inter-caste marriages. Manu specified the functions of these mixed-castes rigidly. These mixed castes originated from inter-caste marriages, which went on ramifying with increasing branches with the advancement of time. For example, among the four basic castes marriages of lower-caste males with upper caste females may create 6 inferior castes, from these 6 sub-castes, further 120 (5x4x3x2x1) sub-castes may be generated by inter-caste marriages and so on. The sub-castes mentioned by Manu include:

Ahindika, Ambashthas, Andhra, Antyāvasāyi, Āyogava, Candāla, Dāsa, Dasyu, Dhigvanas, Kaivarta, Kārāvara, Kshttrs, Kuňkus, Madgus, Māgadhas, Maitreyaka, Mārgava, Meda, Nisāda, Pāndusopāka, Pukkasa, Sairandhra, Sopāka, Sūtas, Ugras, Vaideha, Vaidehaka, Venas.

Functions of some mixed castes

10/32: A Dasyu begets on an Ayogava [woman] a Sairandhra, who is skilled in adorning and attending [his master], who, [though] not a slave, lives like a slave, [or] subsists by snaring [animals].

10/33: A Vaideha produces [with the same] a sweet voiced Maitreyaka, who, ringing a bell at the appearance of dawn, continuously praises [great] men.

10/34: A Nisada begets [on the same] a Margava [or] Dasa, who subsists by working as a boatman, [and] whom the inhabitants of Aryavarta call a Kaivarta.

10/36: From a Nisada [by a woman of the Vaideha caste] a Karavara, who works in leather; and from the Vaidehaka [by the women of the Karavara and Nisada castes] an Andhra and a Meda, who dwell outside the village.

10/37: From a Candala by a Vaideha woman is born a Pandusopaka, who deals in cane; from a Nisada [by the same] an Ahindika.

10/38: But from a Candala by a Pukkasa woman is born the sinful Sopaka, who lives by the occupations of his sire, and is ever despised by good men.

10/39: A Nisada woman bears to a Candala a son [called] Antyavasayi, employed in burial grounds, and despised even by those excluded [from the Aryan community].

10/40: These races, [which originate] in a confusion [of the castes and] have been described according to their fathers and mothers, may be known by their occupations, whether they conceal or openly show themselves.

10/47: To Sutas [belongs] the management of horses and of chariots; to Ambashthas, the art of healing; to Vaidehakas, the service of women; to Magadhas, trade.

10/48: Killing of fish to Nisadas; carpenters' work to the Ayogava; to Medas, Andhras, Kunkus, and Madgus, the slaughter of wild animals.

10/49: To, Ugras, and Pukkasas, catching and killing [animals] living in holes; to Dhigvanas, working in leather; to Venas, playing drums.

10/50: Near well-known trees and burial-grounds, on mountains and in groves, let these [tribes] dwell, known [by certain marks] and subsisting by their peculiar occupations.

10/51: But the dwellings of Candala and Svapakas shall be outside the village, they must be made Apapatras, and their wealth [shall be] dogs and donkeys.

10/52: Their dress [shall be] the garments of the dead, [they shall eat] their food from broken dishes, black iron [shall be] their ornaments, and they must always wander from place to place.

All these castes have been assigned the most difficult, risky and dirty tasks and considered as untouchables and to reside far away from the mainstream of the four basic castes. Here we find the origin of the dalits and the basis of their social, economic and political exploitation.

Now let us go into the psychosis of these prescriptions. In fact, the caste or varna system was theoretically considered to be a kind of social division of labour and castes were to be determined not by birth but by skills and qualities. But the caste system as existed in reality [and sanctified by Manu] was based on heredity and was the most important instrument of exploitation of the majority by the minority. With economic progress and multiplicity of economic activities sub-castes were required for this purpose and inter-caste marriages created this opportunity. So, in India the caste system was a covert form of slavery and the most powerful method to perpetuate surplus extraction by kings, priests, warriors, businessmen and landlords. This psychosis is also the basis of modern capitalism and without eliminating this basic psychosis of exploiting the majority, we cannot meaningfully empower the dalits and other exploited classes.

Explanation from Sankhya Philosophy

According to Sānkhya Philosophy1 human consciousness is a part of material manifestation of Nature and it is the combination of three modes viz. satva, rajas and tamas, endowed by Nature2. All these basic modes combine in different degrees to assign different characteristics to different individuals. If isolated in the abstract, unmixed satva pertains to goodness and virtue, rajas to passion and insatiable desire and tamas to darkness of mind, obsession and inertia. All our mental and intellectual faculties originate from these three basic modes (Ballantyne 1885: I.61, I.125-27, I.141, II.27). Accordingly people may be classified broadly into three major categories:

(i) tāmasika (dominated by tamas mode); (ii) rājasika (dominated by'rajas' mode); and (iii) sātvika (dominated by satva mode). Sātvika people are characterized by nobler qualities (like abstinence, self-sacrifice, love, philanthropy, mercy, self-confidence, diligence, and composure etc.) whereas rājasika and tāmasika people possess various combinations of baser qualities (like greed, envy, hatred, anger, selfishness, lust, idleness, cruelty, and pride etc.) (Basu 2005)

The sacred Hindu scripture Gītā describes in detail the various aspects of these basic attributes (14.05-09, 14.11-13, 14.16, 14.17, 17.12, 17.18, 17.19 -22, 18.20-39, Telang 1882). A sātvika person is free from egotism, seeks knowledge of self and the eternal, performs duties unselfishly and without attachment (i.e. without desire rewards or fruits of the activities and unperturbed by success or failure), is full of resolve and enthusiasm. A rājasika person is activated by material desires (for wealth, power, sensual pleasures etc.) and attached to his works (too much concerned with the fruits of work), is full of greed and selfishness, egotism, restlessness and excitement over the results of his works. He may undertake austerity, acts of sacrifice and charity, but only to get something in return (revenue, power, social positions etc.) and to make a show off. He cannot distinguish between righteousness and unrighteousness, and right and wrong action.

A tāmasika person is full of inertia leading to ignorance, delusion, slowness of mind, carelessness, laziness, inactivity, excessive sleep, vulgarity, malice. He performs observes austerity with foolish stubbornness with self-torture or for harming others. His head is full of irrational and baseless knowledge, fear, grief, despair, fatalism and he undertakes action out of delusion, disregarding his abilities and loss or injury to others. He is always depressed and procrastinating.

Now let us take up another concept of Hindu philosophy, viz. the concept of ripu. In general ripu means enemies. These ripus in Hindu philosophy are excesses of some basic instincts or reflexes of human mind or intellect. They are necessary for our material existence. So as such they are not enemies. But for beneficial effects they must be balanced and under our control. If they are in excess, they become our enemies or ripus and result in disastrous effects both for us and for the human society. The western scholars often mistakenly translate ripu as sin. But ripus are not sins, rather sources of sins or vices. There are six ripus: kāma (desire for material pleasue/sexual desire/lust), krodha (anger), lobha (greed), moha (infatuation/attachment/obsession), mada (pride/vanity/arrogance), mātsarya (envy).

The ripus take various major forms under different modes.

For sātvika persons they are fully controlled and turn out benign – they reside in such a person in perfect harmony with ethical living.

For rājasika and tāmasika persons, however, these ripus become vicious and harmful for both the individuals and the society. For the former the ripus combine to result insatiable greed and power mongering and to dominate over other persons and society. For the latter, on the other hand, they result in inertia, fatalism and submission to slavery. The rājasika people try to force the majority in to languish in the tāmasika state so as to rule them and build up their economic and social power by enslaving them and extracting their surplus products.

Coming to our context, the people in the upper strata of the society are in the rājasika state and the dalits are forced to be in the tāmasika state through poverty, illiteracy, social customs, false religious beliefs, and legal measures by the state machinery which is being controlled by the rājasika minority. This process of de-humanization of the dalits started long ago to fulfill the greed and power mongering of the rājasika upper strata as is evident from the prescriptions of the Manusmriti.

So solution of the dalit problem lies in lifting the dalits to higher modes from the darkness of the tāmasika state. But without lifting these persons out of the morass of abject poverty, it is not possible to enable them to move on to higher modes. But to this end the first and foremost task would be to infuse some sātvika qualities to the rich and the upper strata. As such, in our society, sātvika values cannot generate among the privileged minority, except among the educated, philanthropic and thoughtful persons in the middle class.

Recently, Amartya Sen has strongly appreciated the role of public opinion and free mass media in ensuring social justice in the democratic countries (Drèze & Sen1989). In this context Sen, however, failed to realize that unless the masses and the media men are made free from tāmasika and rājasika obsessions, they cannot play the cherished roles. In earlier systems in India the rājasika feudal or semi-feudal rulers, the priests, and the businessmen thrived on the economic exploitation (social and political deprivations were necessary to perpetuate the economic exploitation) of the lower tāmasika strata, mainly the dalits. In the era of globalization, politicians and political parties in our country have turned into mere characters in a puppet-show, the operators being the capitalists—now-a- days, the rājasika Multinational Corporations (MNCs), who want to bind the entire world with the chains of slavery. Within the LDCs, the politicians (who themselves are slaves of the capitalists) thrive on slavery of tāmasika masses. This is the democratic world we are living in.

So, the dalits in India could be empowered in the true sense of the term only if it is possible to inculcate sātvika values among both the dalits and their exploiters at all levels. Unless the exploiters themselves are purified, they would never permit the slaves to acquire sātvika values and be free from their clutches. But here we are confronted with a serious problem – it is not possible to effectively inspire the common people with sātvika values unless the rājasika character of greed (for wealth and power) of the exploiters are moderated, which is possible only if the dalits are unified and generate pressure on them.

Simple concessions from above would not solve the basic problem. On the contrary, this may make the deprived dependent on outside help and thereby get further submerged in slavery and tamas. Long ago, Rabindranath had warned against this attitude of helping the common people. At the same time he suggested how sātvika values could be inculcated among the masses. To quote:

"For this reason, the most urgent necessity in our country is not to place begging bowls at their hands, but to make them confident of their own strength, to make them realize that a man united with others is a complete entity, an alienated individual is but a fragment." (Tagore 1986).

On the basis of Tagore's suggestions, the following methods may be adopted for the empowerment of the dalits in India in the era of globalization.

1. Generation of awareness of self respect, power of unity and confidence on their own strength among the dalits to change their fate. All the philanthropic people, organizations and NGOs may accomplish this through formal education and education to generate consciousness among the dalits.

2. The dalits should be made aware that not short term concessions (like reservations etc.) but recognition of their social, political and economic rights as equals of all other classes of people in the country is the only means for their sustainable empowerment. Opportunities and freedom as equals for the inculcation of skill, efficiency and development of their inherent attributes, capabilities and talents rather than concessions should be the basic objective of the policy of empowerment.

3. The dalits should also be made aware that the privileged classes would never permit their recognition as social, political and economic equals unless they are forced to do so through persistent movement of and pressure from the dalits themselves.

4. Stress should be laid on social equality and abolition of castes as recognition of one's identity and social status. To this end the

government should be forced to change the heinous policy of stamping people as lower castes under the guise of reservation. So, the reservation policy should be on economic basis and not on caste basis. In fact all legal recognition of caste distinctions should be abolished and dalits should be treated as dalits or oppressed and not as specific castes so that after change of economic status, grounds for social discrimination on the basis of surnames are completely abolished.

5. The government should be forced to take stringent legal measure to prevent all atrocities and practice of untouchability against the dalits.

6. Humanitarian satvika values should be inculcated among the privileged class, through proper ethical preaching, education, legal measures and above all pressure from the unified dalits.

Notes

1. There are six Vedic philosophies: Nyāya, Vaiśeshika, Sānkhya, Yoga, Mīmāmsā, Vedānta. (Sen, K.M. 1961, PP.78-85).

2. In many English versions sātva is translated as goodness, rajasa as passion and tamasa as ignorance. But these renderings hardly convey the actual connotations of these terms – in fact there is no equivalent terms in English language as the concepts are new to the western world. So it would be judicious to incorporate these words directly into the English language.

References

Ballantyne, James R. (translator) (1885) Sānkhya Aphorisms of Kapila, Trübner & Co., Ludgate Hill, London.

Basu, Ratan Lal (2005) "Why the Human Development Index Does not Measure up to Ancient Indian Standards" in The Culture Mandala (The Bulletin of the Center for East-West Cultural and Economic Studies, Bond University, Australia), Vol.6, No.2, January 2005. [http://www.international-relations.com].

Drèze, Jean and Sen, Amartya (1989) Hunger and Public Action, Oxford India Paperbacks1999, New Delhi, pp. 278-79.

Kangle, R. P. (1986): Kautīliya Arthaśāstra, Part-II [English translation], Motilal Banarasidass, Delhi.

Tagore, Rabindranath (1986) "Samabaya Nīti", in Rabindra Rachanavali, 125th Anniversary Edition, Vol. 14, P.313, Visva-Bharati Publishers, Calcutta (translated from Bengali by the author of this article).

Telang, Kāshināth Trimbak (translator) (1882) The BhagavadGītā, The Sacred Books of the East, Vol.8, Oxford Clarendon Press.

Website-1: [http://www.asiasource.org/asip/dalits.cfm]

Website-2: [http://www.hartford-hwp.com/archives/52a/036.html]

Website-3: [http://www.hartford-hwp.com/archives/52a/071.html]

Website-4: [http://www.foil.org/inspiration/ambedkar/ecoreforms.html]

Website-5: [http://pd.cpim.org/2006/0409/04092006_vsrao.htm]

Website-6: [http://www.indianmuslims.info/news/2006/december/27/indian_muslim/pms_address_at_dalit_minority_conference.html]

Website-7: [http://www.hartford-hwp.com/archives/52a/072.html]

Website-8: [http://www.hartford-hwp.com/archives/52a/074.html]

Website-9: [http://us.rediff.com/news/2005/oct/18franc.htm]

Website-10: [http://www.onlinejournal.com/artman/publish/article_603.shtml]

Website-11: [http://www.deccanherald.com/deccanherald/Apr112004/ac5.asp]

Website-12: [http://dalits.blogspot.com/search/label/India]

Website-13: [http://www.dalitsolidarity.org/html/who_are_dalits.htm]

Manusmriti

Sacred Books of the East, Vol. XXV, edited by F. Max Müller, Oxford Clarendon Press, 1888. [In quotations 4/26 means Chapter-4, śloka-26]

Chapter 4. Public Distribution System in India and Food Security

Introduction

Food insecurity for the poor and vulnerable sections of both rural and urban areas of India, which had been a chronic problem since independence, aggravated alarmingly since the inception of the Economic Reforms in 1991. Slow growth of agriculture in the face of rapid growth of population has no doubt intensified the problem but deeper analysis would reveal that the main cause of food insecurity of the majority of the population in India lies not in supply failure but in increasing unemployment, rapid fall in income of the poor in the rural and urban areas and the miserable failure of the PDS in India.

Since 1951, food production increased almost steadily (except for a few bad years) and overstepped the growth rate of population and the Buffer Stock of the Food Corporation of India (FCI) exceeded the required minimum except for the last few years. Still food insecurity increased during the 1990s although there had been a falling trend during the 1980s.

If we look at the buffer stock position of the FCI we come across a paradoxical situation. On the one hand buffer stock has been more than sufficient till 2006 to meet the requirements. For the last few years it has fallen marginally below the minimum required,

which could be met by food imports. On the other hand intensity of food insecurity of the vulnerable segments of rural and urban population has been continuously increasing ever since the 1990s. The percentage of hungry people fell marginally during the period but absolute number increased considerably.

So it becomes clear that supply deficiency is not the basic cause of hunger and food insecurity of the majority of the population. Historical evidence also shows that famines and food insecurity in India in the past arose not because of supply failure but because of wrong policy of the government. Amartya Sen has shown that during the Great Bengal Famine of 1943, there was no scarcity of food grains (Sen 1999).

After independence India has not experienced any acute food crisis in the form of famine which had been a recurrent catastrophe during the British regime, but we have been inflicted with chronic hunger which has been intensified since the 1990s. Here also the basic cause does not lie in supply deficiency but in wrong policy of the government in two ways. First, the policy of liberalization has resulted in fall of income and employment of the vulnerable segments of population and second, the PDS and other safety measures for the poor have become less efficient. So in brief, the basic reason for the recent increasing trend of food insecurity are:

i) Falling income and employment of the poor

ii) Failure of the PDS

In this article we are going to take up the second factor.

Food Insecurity in India

According to report of the Food and Agricultural Organization (FAO) of the United Nations, number of hungry people in India had been:

1979-81: 261.5 million (38%)

1990-92: 215.6 million (25%)

1998-2000: 233.3 million (24%) (FAO 2002)

From the above data it is found that both percentage and number of hungry people declined in India between 1979-81 and 1990-92, but the absolute number increased between 1990-92 and 1998-2000 (although proportion declined marginally).

The Food Insecurity Atlas prepared by M. S. Swaminathan Research Foundation (MSSRF) used two composite Indices of Food Insecurity (one for rural area and the other for urban area) to show that both urban and rural poor in most of the States in India are afflicted with extreme food insecurity (MSSRF 2003, 2004).

According to a United Nations report (Feb 20, 2009) about 20 percent of the world's 1 billion hungry poor live in India and the number of undernourished in India is increasing. India ranks 94th in the Global Hunger Index of 119 countries and about half of Indian children are underweight. [Website-1]

In a recent study Ranjan Ray has used household calorie intake data from recent National Sample Survey rounds to compose a Prevalence of Under-Nutrition Index. On the basis of this index percentage of undernourished rural household in India rose from 48% at the time of NSS Round 43 (1987-8) to 67% at NSS Round 57 (2001-2); undernourished urban households rose from 37% during the same period (Ray, Ranjan 2008).

Now it would appear a real paradox if we consider the buffer stock position of the FCI sins 1994. This is shown in the following table.

Table-1: Buffer Stock with the FCI

Year (Jan)	Buffer norms [million tonnes]	Actual stock [million tonnes]	Year (Jan)	Buffer norms [million tonnes]	Actual stock [million tonnes]
1994	15.4	22.0	2002	16.8	58.0
1995	15.4	30.3	2003	16.8	48.2
1996	15.4	28.5	2004	16.8	24.4
1997	15.4	27.0	2005	16.8	21.7
1998	15.4	18.3	2006	20.0	18.8
1999	16.8	24.4	2007	20.0	17.4
2000	16.8	31.4	2008	20.0	19.2
2001	16.8	45.7			

Source: Economic Survey, 2000-01 (Table: 5.8, p.92); 2002-03 (Table: 5.12, p.92); 2007-08 (Table. 7.25, p. 179)

The above table shows that actual stock of FCI exceeded the minimum requirement in all the years till 2005. Only for 2006-08 it has been marginally lower than the minimum. In fact the problem does not lie in deficiency in buffer stock but inefficient operation of the PDS, especially the targeted PDS introduced since 1997.

PDS in India and Its Failure

One of the major objectives of the Agricultural Price Policy in India, during the plan period, was to assure steady supply of essential food grains to the consumers, especially the poor, at affordable prices. The objective of the price policy of the government was stated as: "The objective of the Government's food security policy is to ensure availability of food grains to the public at an affordable price. The Public Distribution System, which has existed in the country since the Second World War, strives to meet these twin objectives." (Economic Survey, 1994-95, p.80)

The so called Green Revolution added additional importance to PDS. With the introduction of HIV technology the North Western States like Punjab, Haryana, Western U.P. etc. became the main producers of the major cereals and 4 Southern States, Assam etc concentrated more on cash crops. (Patnaik 2001).

This regional specialization called for administered price and distribution policy by the central government to stabilize prices of food grains. Thus the existing PDS system assumed added importance. The Food Corporation of India (FCI) was established by the FCI Act, 1964 to facilitate procurement of food grains, maintenance of buffer stock and distribution of food grains through fair price shops.

Under the PDS, mainly wheat and rice, the two principal cereal food crops in India, are issued by the Central Government at uniform Central Issue Prices (CPIs) to the States and the Union Territories for distribution under PDS. The FCI procures and issues the crops to the States and the Union Territories. The economic cost of the FCI involves costs for procurement, storage, distribution and wastage of food grains.

The gap, between economic cost of FCI and realization based on the CPIs, is filled by the Central Government through 'food subsidy'.

Till 1996 the PDS in India was universal i.e. essential food grains were distributed to everyone irrespective of level of income. In spite of many flaws, the PDS in India till the 1990s played an important role in stabilization food grain prices over the country and averting food crisis. During the severe drought of 1987-88, the PDS played an important role in averting famine and death from hunger. (Chaturvedi 1994).

During the early 1990s the PDS system was criticized on many grounds. One of the criticisms was its marginal impact (on food security) which was considered to be a function of its universality of coverage. (Nawani 1994)

Moreover, universality of coverage was considered to be a cause of high food subsidy. Structural reform measures in India aimed at reducing revenue deficit and fiscal deficit and reduction of food subsidy was considered as a means to fulfill this objective. So from 1997 the universal PDS was replaced by a targeted PDS (TPDS). The new system attempted to divide the population into two categories: Above Poverty Line (APL) and Below Poverty Line (BPL), the latter entitled to receive food grains at lower prices through the fair price shops.

In fact introduction of TPDS created more problems than it solved and made the public distribution mechanism more inefficient. The most serious flaw lies with the definitions of the poverty line and selection of the BPL population who are entitled to food ration at lower prices (Swaminathan 2003).

The problem may be formalized in the following manner:

Let us define (simulating statistical definition) Two Types of Errors:

First Type of Error

E-I: Wrong Exclusion: This error occurs if those who should have been included are excluded.

Second Type of Error

E-II: Wrong Inclusion: This error occurs if those who should have been excluded are included.

Now under universal PDS, E -II error is likely to be high leading to unnecessary high subsidies. TPDS would exclude those who are included due to E-II. It has been shown by some studies that introduction of TPDS reduced E-II considerably (Dutta and Ramaswami 2001; Misra and Swaminathan 2001). Keeping aside the question of E-I error, reduction of E-II is likely to reduce food subsidies, but the available data gives the contrary indication as in the following table.

Table-2: Food Subsidy

YEAR	SUBSIDY (Rs. crore)	YEAR	SUBSIDY (Rs. crore)
1991-92	2850	2001-02	17494
1996-97	6066	2002-03	24176
1997-98	7500	2003-04	25160
1998-99	8700	2004-05	25746
1999-00	9200	2005-06	23071
2000-01	12010	2006-07	23828

Source: Economic Survey, 2000-01, P.96; 2007-08, Table: 7.27, P.180

The above table shows that cost due to food subsidy has steadily increased even after introduction of TPDS.

Now coming to E-I error, it is found that the TPDS has resulted in alarming increase in this type of error leading to exclusion of a large proportion of the poor and the vulnerable sections because of wrong and erratic method of selection of the BPL category.

According to many studies, there is no scientific criteria for identify the BPL household, the criteria used is arbitrary and varies from State to State. (Patnaik 2003). A study found that over half the proportion of households in the lowest 5% of population did not get BPL cards (Kriesel and Zaidi 1999).

Various studies have shown that the poverty line, which is the basis of dividing APL and BPL population, as defined by the Planning Commission, fails to give a true picture of poverty in India as it excludes many people who should be considered poor (Patnaik 2004, Ray and Lancaster 2005).

According to a United Nations Report (op.cit) the TPDS failed miserably due to lack of adequate data and incorrect definition of hunger. In theory, essentials food grains were to be sold only to those who really needed help, but in practice the TPDS excluded large number of the poor and reclassified them as better off than they actually were. Thus according to the report, the TPDS led to greater food insecurity for large sections of the poor and the near-poor [Website-2].

Some other strong opinions against the TPDS are noted below.

1. After 1991, intense pressure from the IMF and the World Bank to reduce the budget deficit brought first a sharp rise in the PDS price of food grains unmatched by higher prices for farmers, and then the introduction of "Targeted PDS" in 1997. Within ten years all that had been gained over a generation was lost. "Targeting" involved the near-criminal use of indefensible "Poverty Lines" to subject a vast impoverished population to paying prevailing market prices for essentials. Though accompanied by hypocritical expressions of concern for the poor from both World Bank and Indian neo-liberals, targeting was a deliberate and successful attack on the PDS system as a whole [Website-3].

2. According to NSS Report on Public Distribution System and Other Sources Of Household Consumption, 2004-05, 58 per cent of subsidised food grains do not reach Below Poverty Line ("BPL") families, as 22 per cent reach Above Poverty Line ("APL") families, while 36 per cent are sold in the black market. Only 57 per cent of BPL households have ration cards, while the homeless often do not have any. Only 28 per cent of the rural poor have benefited from any type of government food assistance schemes, and for urban areas the figure is just 9.5 per

cent. Over half (51%) of rural households with the smallest landholdings (less than 0.01 hectares) do not possess ration cards that entitle them to monthly rations of rice, wheat, sugar and kerosene under the PDS [Website-4].

Thus we see that introduction of the TPDS since 1997 has failed to reduce E-II error appreciably. On the other hand it has led to alarming increase in E-I error nullifying the basic objective of the PDS to ensure food security for the majority. Moreover introduction of the TPDS has made the rationing system nonviable in many areas of the country. In the new system off-take by the APL population fell drastically. On the other hand off-take by the BPL population also declined due to fall in income. These made the system inoperative in many areas. (Chakravarty and Dand 2005)

Conclusion

From the above analysis we find that the basic causes of food insecurity in India lie not in supply failure but in declining income and employment in the unorganised sector and failure of the TPDS that excludes a large segment of the poor because of definitions and methods of implementation. So far as policy of introducing the TPDS is concerned, it may be said that the policy as such is not unsound but the real problem lies in the way it is implemented. The following guidelines may improve the functioning of the TPDS:

1. Correct definition of the poverty line following international norms and updating definition regularly.

2. Measures for collecting adequate data on the basis of which people below poverty line are to be selected.

3. Measures to improve functioning of the fair price shops removing inefficiency and corruption.

4. Regular supply of essential articles to the fair price shops.

5. Reduction of wastage and other unnecessary costs of the FCI.

6. Bringing the tribal population residing in remote areas under the cover of rationing system.

7. Measures to raise income and employment of the extreme poor through direct poverty removal schemes.

References

Chakravarty, Sujay and Dand, Sejal, A. (2005): "Food Insecurity: Causes and Dimensions", p. 14, <http://ideas.repec.org/p/iim/iimawp/2005-04-01.html>

Chaturvedi, S. (1994): "India Tries for Drought Tolerance", Biotechnology and Development Monitor, No.18, p.8

Dutta, B. and Ramaswami, B. (2001): "Targeting and Efficiency in the Public Distribution System, Case of Andhra Pradesh and Maharashtra", EPW, Vol.36, No.18, May 5, pp.1524-32

FAO (2002): "State of Food Security in the World",

<http://www.fao.org/documents_cdr.asp?url_file=/docrep/005/v7352e/v7352e00.htm>

Govt. of India, Economic Survey, 2000-01, 2002-03, 2007-08

Kriesel, S. and Zaidi, S. (1999): "The Targeted Public Distribution System in Uttar Pradesh, India – An Evaluation", Working Paper, World Bank, Washington DC, August

Misra, N. and Swaminathan, M. (2001): "Errors of Targeting: A case Study of Public Distribution System of Food in a Maharashtra Village, 1995-2000", Ithaca: Mario Einaudi Centre for International Studies, Cornell University

MSSRF (2003): "Food Insecurity Atlas of Rural India", Report of MSSRF and World Food Programme (WFP) of the Food Aid Organization of UNO

MSSRF (2004): "Food Insecurity Atlas of Urban India", Report of MSSRF and World Food Programme (WFP) of the Food Aid Organization of UNO

Nawani, N. P. (1994): "Indian Experience on Household Food and Nutrition Security", FAO Report, Regional Expert Consultation, FAO-UN, Bangkok

Patnaik, U. (2001): “Concentration of Regional Food Output and the Public Distribution System”, People’s Democracy, XXV (23), June 2001

Patnaik, U. (2003): “Food Stocks and Hunger: Causes of Agrarian Distress”, Social Scientist, Vol.32, No.7-8, July-August

Patnaik, U. (2004): “External Trade, Domestic Employment and Food Security: Recent Outcomes of Neo-Liberal Economic Reforms”, Conference (‘the Question of Asia in Global Order’) Paper, Asia Pacific Institute, Duke University, Oct 1-2

Ray, Ranjan (2008): "Diversity in Calorie Sources and Undernourishment during Rapid Economic Growth," EPW, February 23

Ray, R. and Lancaster, G. (2005): “On Setting the Poverty Line Based on Estimated Nutrient Prices: Condition of Socially Disadvantaged Groups during the Reform Period”, EPW, Vol.11, No.1, January

Sen, Amartya (1999): “Food, Economics and Entitlements” in Drèze, Jean, Sen Amartya and Hussain, Arthar (eds), The Political Economy of Hunger, Oxford University Press, New Delhi, pp. 50-68

Swaminathan, M. (2003): “Strategies towards Food Security”, Social Scientist, Vol.31, No.9-10, Sept-Oct, p.58

Website-1: <http://tvnz.co.nz/world-news/indian-food-policy-failing-2497797>

Website-2: <http://tvnz.co.nz/world-news/indian-food-policy-failing-2497797>

Website-3: <http://www.monthlyreview.org/mrzine/amr160508.html>

Website-4: <http://www.cseindia.org/programme/nrml/infocus-august07.htm>

About the Author

The author of this volume Dr. Ratan Lal Basu is a Ph. D. in Economics (on Arthaśāstra, the treatise on political economy and statecraft composed by a Brāhmaṇa scholar Kauṭilya around 300 B. C.). He retired as principal from a Government-Sponsored College at Kolkata, and after retirement got fully occupied with research and publishing activities pertaining to Indology, ancient economics, modern economic problems, economic history, yoga and tantra cult, statecraft, international relations and espionage, ethics and morality and also fiction in English and Bengali (his mother tongue).

www.ingramcontent.com/pod-product-compliance
Ingram Content Group UK Ltd.
Pitfield, Milton Keynes, MK11 3LW, UK
UKHW041821200726
13854UKWH00001BA/428